I0392683

Blockchain

The Complete Guide to Understanding the Technology Behind Cryptocurrency

Table of Contents

Introduction

I want to thank you and congratulate you for downloading the book *Blockchain: The Complete Guide to Understanding the Technology Behind Cryptocurrency.*

This book contains full insight on how to become truly more versed and knowledgeable of how encryption methods work in today's world that almost demands digital shopping and the completion of electronic payments. Once you have read this book, you will have an entirely better understanding of exactly how the Blockchain database technology began through the development of an application called Bitcoin, why the Blockchain method is arguably more important than the development of Bitcoin itself, and the vast implications that Blockchain and cryptographic encryption methods have for our society and economy in the future, both physically and digitally. These discussions will include becoming familiar with concepts such as hashing, the significance of a nonce, and how miners interact to form the success of Blockchain technology as a whole. If these concepts are currently unfamiliar to you, don't panic. By the end of this book you will be ready to easily explain these tricky concepts to other people. If you have never engaged in an online application such as Bitcoin, this book might motivate you to dip your toe into these digital waters.

Here's an inescapable fact: you will need a desire to not get robbed or taken advantage of within the digital financial atmosphere in order to benefit from this book. This book will help you to understand exactly how online transactions are made and how you can keep yourself safe amongst the infinite number of people out in cyberspace who are waiting to take advantage of you.

Additionally, this book will help to give you better knowledge of the algorithms associated with the Blockchain method as well as the infinite places where the Blockchain database technology can lead society and the economy in the future. This book will also discuss how applications such as Bitcoin are expanding how people are interacting virtually. A quick example of this is by using Bitcoin for transactions that go beyond currency. People are using Bitcoin as a way to stake ownership in areas such as property and contracts, and the possibilities for this type of exchange are endless. While this book will explore how exactly the Blockchain method works, it will also explain the countless possibilities that are available now that Blockchain has been well established and verified as nearly impenetrable.

If you do not develop your knowledge of the Blockchain method and its ties to cryptology, you run the risk of being left behind in the information age. Technology such as the Blockchain database structure is reorganizing how people form and establish online business. Without a working knowledge of the concepts presented in this book, how will you be able to safely launch yourself confidently into the world of online shopping and interacting?

It's time for you to become amazingly versed in how Blockchain technology works. Let's get started!

Chapter 1:
Trust, Money, and the Internet

The Origin of Distrust in the Marketplace

A memory that is still painfully etched into anyone's mind who has had stock in the economy in the last ten years is the 2008 economic crisis. While the intricacies on the subject can be complicated, the bottom line is that the big banks preyed upon new homeowners. The mortgage lenders, whom the homeowners trusted, made the homeowners think that they could afford a larger mortgage payment than was possible. The homeowners took out huge loans, of which the banks took advantage, and then when the homeowner realized the inability to keep up with the mortgage payments, he or she went bankrupt. With this being the result of so many new mortgages all over the country, the stock market collapsed. This resulted in jobs being lost, lives being ruined, and overwhelming global economic crisis. To this day, it is argued amongst economists whether or not global trade will ever be the same because of this financial meltdown. During this time, while regular American citizens went broke, the banks were largely unaffected. Some top bank representatives even ended up profiting from the calamity.

Overall, the financial crisis left people feeling tricked and deceived by their banking institutions, and this developed a desperate need for more transparency and trust within banking establishments. Manifestations of this public discontent include the Occupy Wall Street movement and the creation of the term, "the one percent". Because the banks were not heavily fined or punished for their greedy actions, the public still largely does not trust the banks and the banks continue to reap large cash rewards from their customers. These rewards include but are not limited to charging high ATM withdrawal and late fees and other high transaction costs. To some, these fees seem unfair, especially after witnessing how the banks behaved in 2008. Why should they have our trust?

Internet marketplaces have skyrocketed in popularity over the last few years. E-bay, one of the first online consumer forums, now competes with sites such as Etsy, Amazon, and Society6 to generate the most profits from online shopping. Today, it seems as though every store that began as a physical place now also has a shop on the web. Online shopping has revolutionized the way in which people interact with their marketplace. Now all it takes is a couple of clicks and a credit card for a purchase to be made. And that's the problem. While the internet has changed consumerism, consumerism is still monopolized by the dominance of the banking industry. For example, it's impossible to buy a pair of shoes online without owning a credit or debit card. Cash is not an option. The money available on these cards is being funded by a bank somewhere. The trust the consumer needs to have in their bank still exists even though the storefront has gone from physical to digital. The need for a third party to regulate transactions from one person to another has caused some people to stop engaging in online banking. It has caused others to seek to invent ways to purchase goods that bypass the need for a trusted third party that dictates all of the online banking rules. Easily the most popular invention of this kind is Bitcoin.

Trust Given to Everyone

Bitcoin's solution to eliminating greedy banks who gouge their customers through transaction and late fees is to replace the third-party bank with a more democratic system. Instead of one person using the credit from his or her banking institution to complete a transaction that will populate into the bank account of the seller, all transactions in Bitcoin are publicly visible to all users of a database. It will be discussed in the following chapters exactly how Bitcoin has sought to accomplish this, but a major component of their application involves the idea of a Blockchain. The primary goal of a Blockchain is to notify all of the participating users in a given program that a transaction is occurring, and these transactions are documented in a public ledger. Instead of using a third party to negotiate terms between the two people, cryptography is used as a way for everyone to trust the system.

More specifically, the idea of a public ledger is what gives Bitcoin its validity in the eyes of everyone using its system. Every time a transaction occurs in Bitcoin, it is recorded on the public ledger so that everyone can see it at any given moment. This drastically contrasts the traditional forms of banking and accounting since it is typical for banking to be done privately behind closed doors. By recording all transactions on a public ledger, records cannot be discreetly altered by one person. Additionally, there is no single person or corporation that owns the financial information of other people. While the role that miners play in Bitcoin and Blockchain technology will be better explained in subsequent chapters, the principles of cryptography combined with the idea of a public ledger are what give Blockchain technology an air of trust without an individual user subscribing his or her trust to a single person or entity.

Bitcoin's decision to not only transfer trust from financial institutions to something that is completely digital but also create a new type of online currency seeks to entirely bypass a staple of modern financial life since 2000 B.C. when the first bank was created. While there are still currently some bugs that need to be worked out within the Bitcoin application itself, the Blockchain database structure is one that is sound and continues to help secure applications that are both financial and non-financial alike. Since Bitcoin is the most popular type of application that uses Blockchain, understanding Bitcoin is important, but the primary goal of the overall discussion will be to better understand how the Blockchain technology works and the social and economic impacts of Blockchain technology into the future.

Chapter 2:
The Origins of Bitcoin and Why Blockchain Matters

Understanding Bitcoin is the first step in understanding Blockchain because it is the most controversial form of how Blockchain is used and it is also the most popular. Cryptography is also a central piece to the puzzle of Bitcoin, so it will also be discussed in this chapter, as will the concepts of public and private keys. Bitcoin is considered by some to be controversial because it is the only form of online currency exchange that is not federally regulated. While this may seem like a positive for online consumers who want to feel less taken advantage of by big and manipulative banking institutions, it then becomes the responsibility of Bitcoin to make sure that everything on their network is secure. If their network is not secure, Bitcoin runs the risk of having their user's information hacked or otherwise compromised. This need to secure Bitcoin's network is an example of why Blockchain as a technology is immensely important for the internet today.

The Mystery Surrounding Satoshi Nakamoto

The concept of Bitcoin was thought of by a man named Satoshi Nakamoto. In 2008, Nakamoto wrote a paper called, "Bitcoin: A Peer-To-Peer Electronic Cash System". That same year Bitcoin.org was registered to be a domain name. It's interesting to note that this paper was released in 2008, the same year as the international economic crisis. Quickly following up his paper with an actual working program, the first Bitcoin transaction was completed in January of 2009. Unfortunately, while his application showed prowess for success, by 2011 Nakamoto had completely distanced himself with anything having to do with Bitcoin. It seemed as though he had totally disappeared. To this day, no one is certain of who Nakamoto is. While this may seem like it's a detriment for Bitcoin as a whole, there is some commentary surrounding the subject that suggests that the anonymity of Nakamoto compliments the idea of Bitcoin as a whole. This can be explained by examining exactly how Bitcoin operates and what Nakamoto outlined in his paper, "Bitcoin: A Peer-To-Peer Electronic Cash System".

Nakamoto's paper described exactly what Bitcoin is today; an online forum of automated currency that can be traded between individuals without a third-party interfering between the two. It emphasized the responsibility of all the members of the Bitcoin community being aware of all of the transactions that occur within its borders because everyone in the community knows exactly how much of the finite amount of currency is circulating around the community at one time. When thinking about this in relation to the secret nature of Nakamoto, some think that his disappearance makes sense. If Bitcoin had one obvious originator, everyone would go to that one person and have him decide on decisions for the group as a whole. Nakamoto's disappearance coincides with the philosophy and overall design of Bitcoin.

So...What is a Bitcoin? An Introduction to Cryptography

Quite simply, a Bitcoin is a form of digital coinage, also known as cryptocurrency. The user can individually decide how much his or her bitcoin is worth depending on what is being traded at a given time. 1 bitcoin can be divided into any amount of 100.000.000 units, and thus the possibilities are endless in terms of how much value the user wants to give a

Bitcoin. Additionally, a "Bitcoin" is not the unit of currency for each Bitcoin unit. A user can define a Bitcoin to represent a dollar, a yen, a krona, etc. or also expand its value to include units of energy. A bitcoin can even represent stock in a company. Before proceeding into the more technical aspects of Bitcoin privacy and security, it's important to understand that while Bitcoin is considered "digital currency", the design of the program itself is more concerned with preserving the ownership of an individual's digital currency, rather than creating any type of digital currency that resembles a dollar, for example. In this way, a Bitcoin serves as a digital certificate of ownership more than just your average form of currency.

Cryptocurrency can be defined as a form of online currency that maintains its value through certain encryption techniques that are defined through the broader name of cryptography. Cryptographic methods send and receive data in a way that requires the knowledge of specific information in order to prove the owner's identity. There are four main principles that cryptography seeks to maintain. Examples have been given within each element of cryptography in hopes of making the subject more tangible:

1. Concealment. Cryptography seeks for the information being transmitted to only be understood by the person whom ordered or bought the information being sent. It seeks to eliminate any form of information trespassing. A physical example of this type of encryption would be if you had to know a specific password in order to enter a club or private space.

2. Integrity. Cryptography seeks to protect the original content of what is being sent or received. This involves the detection of any attempt that is made to alter

information once it begins the process of being delivered elsewhere. The promise of integrity would be the equivalent of keeping the finalized version of information or money in a padlocked briefcase and giving it to a trusted friend or colleague to be passed onto the final recipient.

3. Transparency. Cryptography seeks to make it impossible for the originator or sender of any type of encrypted information to later reject that he or she is the one who sent the information. Ensuring this helps to keep a network honest. With some sort of record system, people cannot claim that he or she never sent something in hopes of gaining an advantage. An example of this in physical terms could be an authorized letter that requires a certified seal of approval from an important person like the President or a judge, or a more advanced method of identity that requires a fingerprint record in order to complete a transaction.

4. Verification. Cryptography seeks to ensure that both the sender and receiver can confirm the identity of one another as well as confirm the original and final destinations of where the information has been and is going. In making this possible, both parties can be sure that their information (or in the case of Bitcoin, currency) is coming from a trusted source and that it has not been tampered with or stolen in the past. This would be the equivalent of having proof that the diamond you purchased was not a source of conflict or violence in the past.

A derivative of the word cryptography is *kryptos*, which means hidden in Greek. The objectives of cryptography that were defined above are used for not only Bitcoin but also government agencies around the world. Currently, mathematicians and computer programmers who are highly skilled in this area of work compete with one another to break cryptographic codes and develop new ways of making cyber security possible. Bitcoin specifically uses cryptographic methods as a way to replace the trust that people feel in third party banking institutions to complete transactions. How exactly is this accomplished? Let's discuss public-key versus private-key cryptography, as these concepts are essential to eventually understanding how Blockchain facilitates Bitcoin technology.

Private-Key and Public-Key Cryptography

Private-key and public-key cryptography are important in understanding how user-based encryption works. You can think of both private and public keys as being paired with one another. At this point, it is beneficial to use the example of Bitcoin in order to understand this potentially complicated concept.

Every wallet in Bitcoin has a private-key with which it is associated. In order to make a transaction (in this case, in order to transfer Bitcoin cryptocurrency from one person's wallet to another), both the sender and the receiver have to authorize the transaction using a private key. Each Bitcoin wallet contains at least one private key. The private key is the "coupon" that allows a person to spend his or her cryptocurrency. For example, let's say that a Bitcoin user named Emily wants to send 100 Bitcoins to another Bitcoin user named Brian. To secure this transaction, Emily would first send her private key - the one specific to her wallet and this specific transaction - to Brian's public key. Public keys can be described as a shortened version of Brian's Bitcoin address. Think of this as someone's home address. The public knows this home address so that anyone can send Brian mail or invitations, but only Brian can know the specific contents of the messages and invites that he periodically receives.

Once Emily sends her private key to Brian, she is digitally "signing" or giving the rights of her private key to him. Brian then has to accept and verify that Emily has indeed sent him what she claims to have sent him. He can verify this by looking at her public key, her home Bitcoin wallet address, to know that the information she is giving him is valid. More specifically, the public ledger is what actually verifies that Emily's account contains adequate Bitcoin funds. Once Brian is given her private key and knows that her 100 Bitcoins are now his, he can verify that her Bitcoin signature is valid through her public key. Verification of the private key ensures two important features for Bitcoin:

1. It ensures that Emily owns the Bitcoin private key, and thus the amount of Bitcoin that she claims she does. If Brian does not receive the key and cannot verify that the funds exist, there is reason to believe that the transaction is counterfeit.

2. Emily's public key shows all of her transaction history. Through the publication of every transaction that she's ever made and by comparing that to how much Bitcoin she originally had in her wallet, it is easy to confirm that she has the 100 Bitcoins available to give to Brian.

Also important to note; the ability for Emily to give Brian the capability to see and verify the private key for the transaction is called "sweeping". This means that the private key is transmitted to the person receiving the currency and more importantly that a message is sent to everyone who uses Bitcoin that a private key has just been exchanged between two people. While this method does run the risk of the potential for double-spending, (what if Emily sent her private key to multiple people?) the alternative is arguably more dangerous. If Emily were to offer her private key without letting everyone else in the community know, Brian could end up being robbed. This would be like if Emily gave Brian her credit card information but Brian decided to swipe her card after he had already given her the goods. If Emily's credit card is declined or the transaction bounces, Brian is out of money and Emily already has what she intended to buy with no consequences attached.

While it's obvious through the example of Emily and Brian's interaction that Bitcoin successfully created the ability for others to safely send and receive funds with the use of encrypted private keys and the use of public keys, Blockchain seems like it's not part of this equation at all; however, when Bitcoin was first established it had a few problems with its design. Bitcoin programmers developed Blockchain as a way to fix these problems.

Chapter 3:
How Blockchain Put
Everything in Order

The concept of a Blockchain was developed as a way to counter a problem that Bitcoin was having within its system. This problem involved putting the transactions in chronological order. Let's take our example from the previous chapter. While Emily and Brian are agreeing upon terms and finalizing their deal with one another, two people named Mary and Robert are also completing a transaction of a similar nature. It turns out that Emily, Brian, Mary, and Robert all finalize and submit their transactions at the exact same time, 2:03AM. This might initially seem extremely coincidental, but when you consider the breadth of Bitcoin and its worldwide reach, the possibility does not seem that unrealistic. The question for Bitcoin becomes, "which transaction gets recorded into the public ledger first?"

Changing how the public ledger operates helped to fix this problem. The public ledger documents what is being traded at a given time and is sent out to everyone within a network in order to maintain consistency in recordkeeping. Another way to look at this problem is to ask which transaction gets sent out to everyone else in Bitcoin first? If transactions are not put into chronological order, the ability for people to double-spend becomes even greater. For example, if you were looking to burglarize the system and sent one transaction at 2:03AM but this wasn't recorded until 5:04AM, it would look like you still owned currency that was actually already given away. To put this more simply, if multiple transactions are being made simultaneously but are being recorded in a non-chronological way, the accounting of where Bitcoin is being distributed at any given second would be wrong. The public ledger would be wrong and people would not know exactly who owns the Bitcoin. In this way, trust in the system would erode.

Blockchain Basics

To minimize the possibility for multiple transactions to be recorded simultaneously, Bitcoin developed the concept of putting all transactions that are made at the same time to be put into a "block". All of the sequential blocks that are made are linked to one another through a "chain" (hence the name Blockchain) in a chronological order. When a block is recorded on the public ledger, information such as the time and date of the transaction, the participants who are conducting the transaction, and the amount of currency that is being traded is all recorded on the public ledger. While these blocks help to eliminate the problem of not sequencing transactions in a uniform and precise order, there are still questions that need answering. These questions include who is authorizing the blocks from to be integrated into the chain? More importantly, how can it be assured that whoever is authorizing the transactions that are collectively put into the block are not simply creating fake blocks of currency and infiltrating the chain with them? This is where the idea of a miner must be introduced.

The Communication Capabilities of Nodes and the Concept of Mining

A Decentralized Network

One of the most important concepts to understand about a Blockchain database is that it promotes decentralized control. This is also commonly known as the Distributed Consensus Model. Going back to the concept of a bank, traditional banking uses one organization or group of investors who control the flow of cash. Centralizing the control of money, even when a financial institution has multiple physical banks across many states or even the entire country, privatizes the information collected and distributed within its walls. Banks consist of many people who serve as accountants who are constantly and physically calculating numbers to make sure that the account payable and accounts receivable are always in balance. Contrastingly, a Blockchain uses many people located across the world in order to police its database and accounting system. This is done through people who are known as "miners". Miners use their personal computers to verify that each transaction within an entire block is valid and makes sense. In this way, a Blockchain is not only decentralized, it can also be interpreted as a type of distributed network as well. Within Bitcoin, miners are paid a small Bitcoin salary to maintain these mining sites. This incentivizes a miner to act within the parameters of the Bitcoin regulations.

Nodes in Relation to Mining

A node within the terms of the geek world of computer processing and technology can be defined as simply a connection point that facilitates the process of communication. For a network made up of primarily Blockchains, the type of nodes that are used to facilitate communication are known as physical. A physical node network means that there are physical computers that are working to maintain the system, and as was just described the people behind these computers are known as miners. As was previously discussed through the example of Emily and Brian, once a transaction is made, a message is sent out to all the participants within a system that a transaction has been completed. These messages are sent not to the individual users within the system but to the miners who are patrolling the network as a whole. Sending this information out to the miners helps to ensure that everyone is seeing the same transaction taking place. With multiple people verifying that a block of transaction is sound, this leaves less ability for hackers to infiltrate the system with a fake or counterfeit block into the chain.

Now that it's been explained who is patrolling the Blockchain for validity, let's go back to the original problem of having multiple Bitcoin transactions occurring at one time. While the block method helps to keep groups of transactions together, what is to happen if two blocks are submitted to be admitted into the chain at once? How can it be agreed upon by all of the miners at the specified nodes that one group of transactions occurred before or after another? This is where the concept of hashes and nonce numbers become relevant.

Creating Priority Through Puzzles

Once a miner has a group of transactions that occurred within a certain time period, he or she cannot simply submit the block and have it automatically added to the chain. There is still work to be done. While putting individual transactions into a block eliminates a large possibility that multiple transactions will be submitted to a chain at the same time, there still exists a small possibility that blocks will be submitted by the miners at the same time. In order to prevent this less likely but still probable possibility and in order to prove that the block is still valid and secure, the miner then must work through a certain type of algorithmic puzzle. For the Bitcoin system, these puzzles take roughly ten minutes to solve. Let's stop for a moment and take a look at how these puzzles are generally comprised.

Puzzle Composition: The Idea of a Hash Function and the Purpose of a Nonce

Bitcoin specifically uses "hashes" along the nodes of the Blockchain to promote a variety of cryptographic benefits. These benefits include relying on two key hash functions to verify identifiers, public addresses, private transaction signatures, and other justifications. As we've already discussed the function of public and private keys within Bitcoin, understanding broadly how a hash function operates can provide more insight into how it can secure a Blockchain. While there are other cryptographic methods that are used in conjunction with Blockchains to help make databases and forms of online recordkeeping more transparent, hashing is most closely associated with the Bitcoin application and will be discussed as one example of how proof of work functions and its role within the broader Blockchain system.

The key purpose of a hash is that is serves as a "proof of work" function within Bitcoin. Part of the miner's job is to figure out the hash algorithm before others who are also competing to upload his or her block into the chain. More specifically, this is accomplished by first recognizing that the process of creating a Blockchain is to read individual transactions from right-to-left, with the most significant and recent transactions being positioned to the right and the less-significant or later transactions happening on the left of the string. This type of sequencing is known as Little Endian number sequencing and it is important when turning the random sequencing of a Blockchain into something significant and useful. There are two functions that Bitcoin uses takes the random information within a block and turn it into something uniform, something that can be consistently compared to the other blocks that are submitted to the chain at the same time. These are hash functions and have the dual role of not only determining which block is going to be the next in the chain, but also prevents fraudulent miners from uploading and prioritizing blocks of transactions that do not actually exist.

Satoshi Nakamoto, when he created the parameters for Bitcoin, introduced two hash functions to be used within Bitcoin. They are:

1. Hash256(d)=SHA-256(SHA-256(d))

2. Hash160(d)=RIPEMD-160(SHA-256(d))

In these functions, D represents the random collection of bytes of information that the miner submits depending on the transactions within the block. SHA is an abbreviation, which stands for Secure Hash Algorithm. This function has a digest length of 256 bits, whereas the digest length of RIPEMD is 160 bits. RIPEMD is also an abbreviation and stands for Race Integrity Primitives Evaluation Message Digest. As was stated in the beginning of this section, the purpose of solving a hash function is to provide the Bitcoin community with a type of "proof of work" statement. The goal of the miner is to find a nonce. So what exactly is that?

A nonce, by definition is a random number that is only used once. Thus, when uploading a block to the Bitcoin chain, a miner has been tasked with finding a specific and predefined number that's figured out by calculating the hash function and the hash of previous chains within the Blockchain. This means that the miner is required to do these equations multiple times, through a trial-and-error process, until the predefined nonce is found. Not only is this process difficult for even an experienced miner, but it is also confounded with the fact that he or she is racing to find the nonce in the fastest amount of time in comparison with other miners within the network. Now can you see why a miner is financially compensated for his or her mathematical work?

Blockchain and Cryptography: How Blockchain Upholds Cryptographic Principles

The "proof of work" capability that hash functions allow within the Bitcoin landscape coincide with the broader principles of what cryptographic technology and what the Blockchain method seeks to uphold. These were explained in chapter 2. The way in which information is sent to miners for verification and certified through the accounting forum of the public ledger allow individual users of the Bitcoin system to use his or her private key to maintain a sense of security within the transaction between two people, while simultaneously being made public through utilization of the public key. This keeps the integrity of an asset's address intact.

Additionally, the integrity of the Blockchain system as a whole is maintained through the patrolling of the miners and the fact that it is impossible for one miner to upload a block of faulty transactions without the other miners in the network knowing that the information is counterfeit. If there is activity that does not mathematically add up along the operation of a node in one place, the other miners working at other nodes will recognize the activity as inconsistent and sound a hypothetical alarm so that no illegal transactions will occur. In terms of transparency, the two types of hash algorithms that the miners are forced to solve in order to upload a block to the chain ensures that all accounts of activity within the chain are in chronological order. Lastly, the hash functions are also used to verify that the individual users within the system (i.e. Emily and Brian) have the funds that he and she claim. It's important to see how all of the cryptographic principles have been met within the Blockchain method, and seeing these principles at work through an explanation of how Blockchain works through Bitcoin helps to better conceptualize the Blockchain method more fully.

The purpose of this e-book is not to detail how exactly Bitcoin is considered by some authorities to be controversial and wrong when compared to traditional modes of financial operation; however, it can be noted that Bitcoin has been criticized for completely bypassing modern forms of third-party financial banking and account rendering. More important than the controversies surrounding Bitcoin are the paramount facts that make the Blockchain method far more successful and significant than the Bitcoin application that invented it. Through the process of establishing individual transactions as a group within a block so that the chronological order of when each transaction took place is possible, the miners who act as the policemen of the

Blockchain system work to collectively conclude whether or not a transaction should be approved or denied into the already existing chain of blocks. Once the block is approved and added to the chain in chronological order, this becomes a complete and transparent record of exactly what transpired within the walls of the Blockchain network. Currency of any type thus moves from wallet A to wallet B without any interference by a middle man or third party who self-servingly collects a fee for enabling a transaction between two parties. Now the Blockchain method has been broadly explained here and also explained step-by-step previously. The following chapters will discuss in length the extensive implications for the Blockchain method into the future, for both financial and non-financial institutions.

Chapter 4:
Bitcoin and Beyond –
Smart Contracts and Current
Blockchain Implementation

More important than the prowess of Bitcoin is the usefulness of the method that support its success, Blockchain. Upon looking into the reach of Blockchain methodology, it becomes obvious that this method of eliminating a third-party resource between two people who wish to trade goods or services is infiltrating other areas of digital society. The Blockchain method is proving to be useful in all areas that revolve around securing online transactions with other people. While this does include activity within the financial realm, it also expands to include areas of the non-financial nature. Let's take a look at where Blockchain technology is currently making strides, before delving into both financial and non-financial capabilities that are said to be possible in the future.

Smart Contracts

If you have ever gone through the process of buying a house, you understand the multiple processes and people that involve this arduous task. Purchasing a home requires a realtor, a home-insurance agency, a home inspector, and countless other steps in order to be considered complete. The paperwork involved is equally intimidating and daunting. Instead of going through each person and process one at-at-time to ensure that each part of the process has been adequately completed, what if there was a way to simply check each step off, and have the process of owning a home be completed without having to physically go to a realtor's office with lawyers, insurance agency representatives and realtors all present? This is what Smart Contracts seeks to accomplish, and it does so primarily through the distinct process of Blockchain methodology. Let's take a look at how Smart Contracts got started, how it works, and how it benefits from the concepts found in Blockchain technology.

In 1994, a man named Nick Szabo conjured up the idea of the Smart Contract, a platform that would allow contracts to automatically exist between people without the need for physical paperwork or milestones. The idea was that once the conditions were adequate and within the parameters of the contract, that is when the contract would begin. Back in 1994, the only problem was that there was no type of way for this transaction to occur because the notion of cryptocurrency did not yet exist. Once cryptocurrency and the Blockchain method came into existence, the Smart Contract was able to flourish. Today, companies are using Smart Contracts in conjunction with cryptocurrency systems like Bitcoin so that people can pay for contractual services without needing a third party. Two companies that currently use Smart Contracts are Codius and Ethereum. Both of these companies use Blockchain in order to implement the contracts.

The Smart Contract operates similarly to how Blockchain works on Bitcoin. While it is much more complicated than this, the Smart Contracts are pre-written with logic that decides how and when a customer is charged because of compliance with or incompliance with a contract. This is accomplished through computer programming including functions. The computer is essentially telling itself, "if this happens, then this is the next step". Once the code has been written, it is stored, replicated and sent out to all of the other nodes along the Blockchain. This is to ensure that everyone policing the network has the same information regarding what should happen when a given circumstance occurs within the contract. Then, when a transaction within the contract does occur, the miners can all approve or deny the request before it gets processed along the chain and written to the public ledger.

The Advantages of Using a Smart Contract

The Smart Contract is important because it can bring to the Blockchain dependable calculations that are relied upon by all users within a network. There are also advantages to using a Smart Contract instead of traditional contractual practices. If the example of operating a bank account is analyzed, it is easy to see how these advantages manifest themselves through the implementation of online contracts. Most people have a debit account, where money is automatically taken out of the account when the card is swiped. This contrasts a credit card, which uses money that the credit card holder does not actually prove ownership of at the time of purchase. There are two primary advantages to Smart Contracts compared to traditional contractual methods that are specifically because of the fact that Smart Contracts use the Blockchain method of processing. These advantages can be interpreted as being in addition to the advantages of Blockchains in general, primarily when considering the benefits and capabilities of cryptography.

1. More efficient monitoring. As was discussed in previous chapters, while an individual owns a bank account, the central proprietorship of the account and its activity is owned by a single banking institution. If you have ever owned a debit card, it is likely that you have experienced having a conversation with your bank about seeing charges on your debit account that you

yourself did not make. These are mistakes. Either the vendor at a restaurant or a store incorrectly charged your card, or someone took your information and is making fraudulent charges. If your bank account was not linked to a single institution but instead to a Blockchain, more people would be looking at your account and approving or denying transactions based on mathematical principles of coding. It would be less likely that an individual could hack into your account because more people are monitoring your activity. With more steps necessary in order to approve a charge, it is impossible, theoretically, to cheat the system.

2. Transparency. As with Bitcoin, Smart Contracts are transparent because they allow everyone in the system to see the code that is working within the contract. Additionally, anyone who thinks that he or she could benefit from using the code is able to use it. While some of the contracts are general and can be easily included in people's lives, others are very specific and cannot be used by everyone. It should be understood that while it may seem positive that everyone is able to see what is happening in the network, lack of privacy is an ongoing criticism of not only Smart Contracts but Blockchains in general. For example, if privacy in banking is something that you value, a Blockchain system of banking might be a service that you avoid because of the public nature of the service.

While there is not much of a negative aspect to having multiple people monitoring and approving transactions on a bank account or any other type of account requiring a contract, transparency can be interpreted as a negative if an individual is seeking traditional forms of privacy in regards to money; however, even if an individual prefers to negotiate contracts privately, having the choice between whether or not to engage in a type of system is an innovation in itself. When thinking about situations such as the housing crisis of 2008 and other types of situations where banks seem to get the best of their customer, it is somewhat comforting to know that maybe someday a customer will have the option of using an exclusively Blockchain operated bank.

A Note on Open Source Companies

Companies such as Ethereum and Codius, which are offering Blockchain software to their customers describe themselves as "open source". This simply means that all of the code that they produce is available to their customers. The big premise of open source companies is that the user has more freedom to use all of the transparent information available within the software to the extent that he or she wishes. In addition to all of the resources of the software being available to the customer, Ethereum in particular is unique because this platform allows a user to create his or her own currency. While the "ether" is Ethereum's form of cryptocurrency, which is what users pay with in order to be a member within Ethereum's system, the company also allows users to create his or her own currency. Similar to Bitcoin, seeing this capability manifest in other companies that are structured in a decentralized way gives credence to the idea that the Blockchain method is changing the way in which business entities are understood and designed. The open source model of operating a business is one innovative way that Blockchain has influenced the understanding of business conceptualization as a whole, and provides private citizens with more diverse options in a variety of ways.

Smart Contracts are currently being used in conjunction with Bitcoin and other types of cryptocurrency as a way to automate contractual obligations between two parties. Because of Blockchain, Smart Contracts are slowly allowing companies to use less resources and find more efficiency within their businesses. The result is happier customers and more accuracy. While the advantages to Smart Contracting include vaster monitoring of accounts and broader transparency, the idea of how much privacy someone deserves within a Blockchain system is still being discussed. Overall, the Smart Contract module as a whole is proving that the Blockchain method is making real and significant developments in the technological business world. While this chapter focused on how the Blockchain methodology is currently being implemented, the next chapters will focus on the potential for Blockchain to grow in both financial and non-financial ways in the future.

Chapter 5:
The Potential for Blockchain Growth within the Financial Sector

While an example of how a debit card banking system would work within the framework of Blockchain technology was explained in the previous chapter, even more significant examples exist of how people have discussed using Blockchain databases and forms of financial record keeping in the future. The most significant types of these include the desire to create a decentralized form of stock exchange. This idea will be discussed at length in this chapter, as well as how Blockchain would improve productivity and overall customer satisfaction. While there are advantages to this process, there are also potential disadvantages that need to also be understood.

Blockchain and the Stock Market

Currently, it is very costly to take a private company and have it publicly listed so that stock in the company can be traded on the stock market. For example, in order to get registered with the New York Stock Exchange, a company must meet several criteria. Firstly, the company seeking entry into the stock market must fill out an application. While there are many aspects to this application, the primary point of the application is that the company applying is promising to adhere to the principles and rules of the New York Stock Exchange. It also offers a company description so that the New York Stock Exchange can become familiar with the company who seeks registration. Secondly, the company must prove that it has at least 400 shareholders in the company, all who collectively own more than 100 shares of the company. The company must also have over one million dollars of the company being publicly traded before entry, and must have a public market share of at least forty million dollars. One last tangible requirement that companies that want to be exchanged on the New York Stock Exchange must comply with is that it must prove that it has made at least ten million dollars in profit for three consecutive years, before tax. Even if all of these criteria (and more) are met by the company that wants to be traded publicly on the New York Stock Exchange, the New York Stock Exchange still has the ability to deny the company entry for a variety of reasons. For example, one reason why a company might be denied entry into the stock market even though it meets all of the initial standards for entry is that the New York Stock Exchange feels that the company in question is not designed or suitable to be traded in an auction-like style. These conditions that must be met are extensive and gaining entry can be exhausting. What if it was easier for a company to start trading on forums such as the New York Stock Exchange? Blockchain has the potential to make this possible.

A New Type of Exchange

Blockchain technology has brought to question the idea of one entity monitoring and accepting or denying a company entry into a system of stock exchange. If a type of exchange program were to be designed that relied solely on Blockchain methods, a single form of authority would cease to exist. Instead, the "miners" who verify whether or not transactions are valid along the Blockchain would be brokers. The brokers would perform the same role of patrolling the Blockchain network as a whole, but they would have a more in depth understanding of finances and how stock exchanges are made. When the public ledger was sent out to each of the brokers along the network, details that would be recorded would include who is buying and selling the stock, how much is being traded, and what time the exchange took place. While an entity such as the New York Stock Exchange would still exist to create rules for the stock exchange operation as a whole, entry into the network would be monitored by programmable codes that could calculate whether or not a company was prepared to enter the market. This would have the potential to result in more consistency within who is accepted and not accepted into the market. The market as a whole would be less able to keep outlier companies from joining the stock market because the rules surrounding who can come in and who can't would be more autonomous than previously.

Decentralizing the stock market in this way would open avenues of public stock trading in a variety of ways. Let's take a look at some of these benefits before focusing on some potential disadvantages.

Advantages of a Blockchain-Oriented Stock Market

A substantial advantage that would exist if the stock market were to adopt a system involving Blockchain methods would be less personnel and resources being required to ensure that stocks are being traded fairly. For example, there would not be a need for auditors to validate a trade between two people because the third-party layout of the market would be replaced with brokers working as miners at each node in the system. The system would also not have to pay employees to verify that the owner of an account has the amount of money that he or she claims before making a transaction because the public ledger would serve this purpose.

Requiring less personnel in order to run a successful stock market system would result in lower transaction costs for the individual users who are engaging in trade. If an individual had more money due to lower transaction costs, it would be possible that he or she would invest more money in the stock market itself, ensuring stability for market as a whole. Additionally, the transactions would occur faster because peer-to-peer confirmation of account activity takes less time than does coordinating communication between people within different departments. Transactions occur much slower today. For example, in the Australian Securities Exchange (ASE) it generally takes three days for a transaction to be completed. During these three days after an individual buys a share, the employees of the Exchange are doing exactly what a Blockchain would do; verifying that the individual is in fact the owner of the account as well as making sure that the individual has sufficient funds to make the deal. If this pace could be quickened, the currency within the stock market would act more like money than it currently does. Cryptocurrency, or ownership of a stock, would be exchanged as quickly as paper money is traded. With stocks having the characteristic of more liquidity, it is possible that individuals would feel more secure in making trades. This could stimulate growth within the market because an individual would feel more like he or she is spending money with a credit card and less like he or she is making a transaction with the heavy term of "investment" attached to it.

Lastly, one other advantage that that would exist in this new version of the stock market would be less fraud. Of course, by this time you are well aware of the fact that the decentralized nature of the Blockchain largely prevents the ability to falsify blocks of information and insert them into the chain, but for the stock market this would be extremely important and useful. There are countless examples of people and corporations attempting to scam the stock market system. When this happens, not only does the system itself lose credibility, but individuals who trust their financial advisors lose vast amounts of money. For example, in 1986 a man named Barry Minkow started a fake company called ZZZZ Best Inc. He figured out to coerce people into investing in his carpet cleaning company, but did not actually plan on giving money back to his shareholders. ZZZZ Best Inc. accrued over two-hundred million dollars before being busted, and Barry Minkow spent twenty-five years in jail. Another type of stock market fraud can be demonstrated through the story of a company called Centennial Technologies. In 1996, the owner of this company, Emanuel Pinez, falsely reported that his company made over two-million dollars in revenue for a given pay period. He had his employees create fake documents to "prove" that this revenue was truly generated. Over time, Centennial Technologies falsely reported roughly forty-million dollars in revenue.

Both types of fraudulent activity could theoretically be prevented by the implementation of Blockchain methods. In the case of ZZZZ Best Inc., having certain code programmed into the Blockchain would diminish the ability of people to create fake companies that looked real. The verification process would be similar to the hash functions that exist within the Bitcoin system, making it relatively difficult to enter the system without the correct type of information. Additionally, in the case of Centennial Technologies, the instantaneous way in which verification of funds would take place along the Blockchain would eliminate any one user's ability to claim that more funds exist in his or her account than actually is true. After understanding both of the examples provided, it becomes obvious that there are a great number of advantages to adopting a Blockchain network for stock marketing purposes. Now that the advantages to switching to a Blockchain-oriented stock market are understood, let's take a look at some of the disadvantages.

Disadvantages Involved in Adopting Blockchain for the Stock Market

If there were no challenges involved in creating a Blockchain for the stock market, then this type of system would probably exist and would have replaced our current system of financial trading. The first disadvantage involves the process of how miners, or in this case, brokers, are paid for their services as the watchdogs for the system. In Bitcoin's version of the Blockchain, the miners are motivated to process the transactions of sales between two people through competition. An aspect of how a miner prioritizes which transaction gets processed first involves being offered different amounts of currency and be given hash function puzzles that are comprised of varying difficulty. If this type of system were to be copied and utilized for the stock market, it would almost be as if the brokers would be bribed to process the transactions in a certain order or preference. This would become especially complicated if a broker at a certain node was influenced by a particular company to operate in a way that somehow created an ability to influence the chain through political bias. While the Blockchain would certainly help to eliminate the successful implementation of bias of this kind, the motivation to bribe a broker would still exist for the individual making a transaction.

Another potential problem for Blockchain and the stock market is the idea of transparency. While the public ledger in general is touted for its ability to create transparency and allow for an individual to have complete information about the system before acting, this type of system would expose types of investors that use anonymity to their advantage. For example, there is one type of investment called a super fund where a large sum of money is gradually sold over a long period of time. If the Blockchain system were adopted for the stock market, an individual could identify this type of transaction within the public ledger. All he or she would have to do is look for patterns within transactions. If he or she noticed that transactions were being made every three months, or every two weeks, etc. then he or she would know when to expect this activity and this would influence his or her spending. Transparency of this kind, within the stock market, might not be desirable.

As you can see, there are both advantages and disadvantages to establishing Blockchain database technology to deal with stock market exchanges. While Blockchain would be able to tackle potential dangers such as the creation of fake companies and prevent a person from claiming that he or she has more funds than is the reality, it could also create a vacuum for brokers to engage in securing transactions with the promise of financial gain through bribes. Transparency is also another aspect of the Blockchain that may initially seem advantageous but within the realm of the stock exchange may not be a benefit but rather a real problem. While this chapter focused on possibilities that exist within the financial sector for Blockchain databases, the next chapter will focus on non-financial possibilities for the Blockchain platform.

Chapter 6:
Blockchain Possibilities within the Non-Financial Sector

It is obvious why Blockchain technology and currency have been discussed together at length. Blockchain began as a way to implement the transaction of currency between two people, and serves as a mechanism of trust within a complicated web of an online marketplace; however, using Blockchain for currency is simply the tip of the ice burg in terms of its utilization capability. As was seen in chapter 4 through the discussion of Smart Contracts, there are ways to use Blockchain techniques without necessarily associating the cryptocurrency with a form of money. This again is done by expanding the possibilities of cryptocurrency to be used as a form of ownership rather than as strictly as a tool used to trade and purchase goods. Code can be programmed along the chain that connects each block so that certain parameters are met. Let's look at a few ways that Blockchains can be used as a form of certifying the authority of documents, property, and cloud-storing capabilities.

Blockchain and Notarizing Digital Documents

If you've ever had to get a document notarized, you know that it can sometimes be a tedious and inconvenient task. If you do not know anyone who is a notary, this means you have to travel somewhere and have your document authorized and stamped in a public place, for example a library or municipal building. Blockchain technology enables an individual to have a document notarized without traveling anywhere, and also ensures anonymity for both the individual's identity and the documents that the individual wishes to get notarized. This eliminates the need for a physical signature of notoriety and aids in proving the following:

1. Who authored a document

2. When the document was authored

3. That the documentation was never tampered with or altered

In addition to proving information about a document, the decentralized network of the Blockchain makes the moving of documents more efficient through digital transfer and decreases potentially high notarization fees. Two useful online companies that are currently using Blockchain methods to certify documents are Block Notary and Stampery.

Blockchain and the Music Industry

The examples of musicians being taken advantage of by their producers are widely known and vast. Movies have been made about the manipulation that goes on in the music industry, and the source of the manipulation usually stems from the musician not properly understanding the jargon within his or her legal contract. Additionally, the rise of the internet and the prevalence of music streaming services, such as YouTube and Spotify, make ripping music from the internet and downloading the music for free easier than ever before. While the days of LimeWire and Napster seem to be largely over, music can still be illegally downloaded in a variety of ways. Blockchain can help a musician in a multitude of ways. Firstly, if processes like Smart Contracting were etched along the chains within the Blockchain, the music royalties for the artist would be better protected and uniform. For example, let's say that one artist chooses to use one specific type of Blockchain exclusively for all of his or her contracts. Instead of having to sift through a contract each and every time he or she makes a new deal, over time the artist will know the main points of the contract and Blockchain design and feel more secure in signing with a new producer or label. Additionally, if the contents of a contract were made public to everyone in the network, it would be harder for the producer to take advantage of an up and coming musician because multiple people would have to approve the contractual transaction before it was implemented.

Decentralized Storage

Another way in which Blockchain is being used is by promoting the use of cloud-based document storage solutions online. Instead of having concrete files shared in one spot, with the files never being duplicated unless the owner of the documents makes it so, having multiple people watching the documents creates more privacy and less intrusion. Similar to how Bitcoin operates, some file storage technology provides monetary incentives for correctly solving puzzles in order to prove that a particular file in question is still available and intact. In addition to file security, another option that opens up with the introduction of Blockchain to decentralized storage is the ability to share unused storage space. Imagine that you own a storage unit, but you don't have enough stuff to fill it up. Instead of settling on wasting valuable space, you decide to rent it out to another person who pays you to use the space. The same is possible virtually when Blockchain methods are applied to cloud based storing systems. Individuals within the Blockchain network are able to share internet bandwidth and even extra space on his or her hard drive in exchange for cryptocurrency. The nonexistence of a central authority over the documents, pictures and other types of data eliminate the possibility of system outages or failures and also increases the ability to control data and stabilize security and privacy capabilities. Of course, the biggest challenge to this type of filing system is making sure that you can trust the people within the network. If you trust someone with your documents, there is still a real chance that the person could deface, resell, or delete something that holds value to you. One great example of a virtual storage bin that implements Blockchain principles is called Storj. If this type of storage is something you would be interested in trying, make sure to check out what Storj has to offer.

Understanding just a couple of ways that the organizational methods of Blockchain can be used that go beyond the financial capabilities is good proof of the fact that this technology has not yet hit its stride. Other ways in which Blockchain can be used non-financially include creating solutions to counteract digital counterfeiting, promote censorship, and help grow the Internet of Things (IoT) community. You now have a good understanding of how Blockchain is used for both financial and non-financial activities alike. While these are optimistic avenues of discussion, there are less pretty aspects of Blockchain. The next chapter will discuss the potential risks associated with using Blockchain.

Chapter 7:
The Risks Associated with Transitioning to a Blockchain Database

While Blockchain database systems represent an exciting and new way to execute tasks quickly and with more efficiently, this innovation comes with its own unique set of problems and potential dangers. It is important to understand the risks associated with this type of database so that steps can be more carefully taken in the future if and when the time comes for more organizations to adopt Blockchain doctrine. Let's briefly take a look at 6 risks that have been discovered within our topic of discussion. Doing so will keep you better prepared for any and all technological innovations that are developed in the future.

1. Trust in the Internet. With credit card fraud and identity theft being real and significant problems in today's digital society, trusting the internet may not be something that currently sits well with everyone. As applications move from being physical to being digital, it will take time for people to realize that electronic transactions are secure, safe and whole. As more and more investments are made into Blockchain database systems and more and more companies move towards being organized in this manner, the customer-employee relationship will change. While everyone hopes that these changes are for the better, the potential exists for change to take time, and trust in the validity of online transactions to come later rather than sooner.

2. The Size of a Blockchain. The extensive nature of a Blockchain in its current form will make it hard for

people to adopt it quickly and easily. Imagine if you were to attempt to participate in a Blockchain network for the first time. You would have to download all of the Blockchain that has been recorded on the public ledger up until that point, and you would have to validate yourself before any transactions could take place. Because of the number of blocks in a chain increase at an exponential rate, this process could take hours or even days to complete. The idea of scaling would have to be addressed within the structure of a Blockchain if this technology were to be implemented on a personal and user-friendly level.

3. Document Conversion. Imagine if a divorce lawyer wanted to move to a Blockchain system so that she could perform divorces more quickly. Before this would be possible, she would have to convert all of the marriage files that are in paper form over to a digital form before embarking on this new type of documentation capability. This would not only take a significant amount of time, especially if the company was large, but it would also take resources and money in order for this process to be successful. The cost of document conversion would have to somehow be address and lowered so that companies could do this with at least relative ease.

4. Public Policy and Lobbying. As Blockchain companies become more and more prevalent, the reality exists that companies that sell and promote alternative business structures that stress a centralized trusted third-party source will try to stop the progress of the decentralized companies. Lobbying efforts within the United States government could slow down the progress of these innovative techniques. Additionally, government

agencies may seek to better more heavily regulate the operations within popular Blockchain networks. While this could provide a benefit in the sense that more people might begin to trust Blockchain methods faster, it could also walk a thin line to becoming regulated in a way that discredits the very heart of the decentralized technology.

5. Currency Trafficking. Although the typical depiction of thieves and thugs do not typically involve images of computers and knowledge of data processing, Blockchain could facilitate processes associated with cryptocurrency trafficking. Especially if it becomes possible to make transactions as fast as it does to exchange money, sophisticated computer thugs could potentially use a Blockchain method of exchange for bad. That being said, if digital governance got to a point where regulations were sufficiently in place and consequences were built in for when someone violated the rules of a network, this could serve to keep the thieves at bay.

6. Cryptographic-Cracking Methods. As technology continues to advance, the possibility exists that devices and de-encryption methods will become available that can easily solve hash functions and other types of puzzles that are used to incentivize miners. Imagine a computer instead of a human miner who solves a function by doing an equation over and over again. This is what a human does now, but it takes a human on average ten minutes to successfully de-encrypt a function. It is possible in the future that computers will exist that will be able to solve certain functions within the Blockchain in a matter of seconds through the principles of quantum computing.

All of these risks – adequate trust, the size of a Blockchain, the stresses of document conversion, the need for proper governance, the likelihood of currency trafficking and digital de-encryption techniques all threaten the way in which Blockchains will be able to thrive in the future. These risks more broadly explain that while Blockchain technology is innovative and promising, there are still plenty of aspects of the structure that need to be worked out and fixed. As technology develops and people become more versed in these types of systems, having an understanding of the risks involved will be crucial to guaranteeing that safe transactions are made. People will adapt to the learning curve needed to successfully navigate this type of technology, and you can only do yourself a favor by choosing to grow along with the pace in which the curve is being met.

Conclusion:
Economic Implications for the Future

Thank you again for downloading this book!

I hope this book was able to help you to better understanding everything there is to know about Blockchain. To reiterate, Bitcoin was the platform that created Blockchain because of a need to chronologically order transactions within its system. Blockchain has various methods in place to uniformly dictate how transactions are processed and seen by the network as a whole through the use of miners, hash functions, and public ledgers. If there is one aspect of the Blockchain database system to remember, it is that Blockchain emphasizes a decentralized system where no one person or entity has control over the network. This change in business model design has the ability to transform how people make transactions without the need of a middleman or third-party participant.

Additionally, it is important to consider that while Blockchain has given people the ability to make processes more efficient and potentially downsize a company, a mass adoption of Blockchain by many companies at once could lead to less jobs or an economic downturn. As was discussed in the beginning of this book, the housing crisis of 2008 marked an extremely distrustful time between financial advisors and their customers. Our analysis of how the stock market would react to the Blockchain method suggests that perhaps a better way to look at Blockchain in the future is to find individual functions that work for specific industries, rather than implementing the Blockchain method without customizing it at all. This way, the Blockchain-related issues that exist within each industry might become smoothed out.

The next step is to experiment with Bitcoin (if you have not already done so) in order to gain some experience with Blockchain systems. If you're already using bitcoin, consider trying another application that runs on a Blockchain system and compare its usefulness to Bitcoin. The knowledge from this e-book will help you to be more aware of how to navigate this potentially complex system, has given you a working knowledge of the terms and processes within the Bitcoin Blockchain, and has also prepared you to identify potential risks that exist within any digital marketplace.

Finally, if you enjoyed this book, please take the time to share your thoughts and post a review on Amazon. It'd be greatly appreciated!

Thank you and good luck!

www.ingramcontent.com/pod-product-compliance
Lightning Source LLC
Chambersburg PA
CBHW071829200526
45169CB00018B/1275

* 9 7 8 1 5 3 7 7 5 3 7 9 9 *